My First Book
Of
Bible Stories

Introduction

Welcome, young readers, to an exciting and enchanting journey through the pages of the Bible! In this special book, we will explore the most beloved stories from the Bible, filled with adventure, wisdom, and valuable life lessons.

As you turn each page, you will meet extraordinary characters like Noah, Moses, David, and many more. Through captivating storytelling and vibrant illustrations, their remarkable tales will come to life before your eyes. You will witness miracles, hear prophecies, and experience incredible acts of faith and courage.

"My First Book of Bible Stories" is designed especially for you, young explorers, to introduce you to the wonders of the Bible in a way that is engaging and easy to understand. Each story has been carefully selected and retold with simplicity and clarity, ensuring that the message shines through.

Through these stories, you will learn timeless values such as love, kindness, forgiveness, and the importance of faith. As you immerse yourself in these narratives, you will discover the beauty and power of the Bible's teachings.

Whether you are reading these stories on your own or sharing them with your family and friends, "My First Book of Bible Stories" is here to ignite your imagination, inspire your heart, and nurture your spirit. It is a treasure trove of wisdom and inspiration that you can return to again and again.

So, open the pages of this magical book and prepare to embark on a wonderful adventure. Let the stories of the Bible capture your imagination, ignite your curiosity, and guide you on a path of discovery and growth.

Are you ready to explore the rich tapestry of the Bible's stories? Let's begin this incredible journey together!

Noah and the Great Flood

The story of Noah and the Great Flood is found
in the book of Genesis in the Bible. It begins
with the wickedness and corruption of
mankind on the earth. God saw how wicked
humanity had become and decided to bring a
great flood to cleanse the earth.

God found Noah, a righteous man, and instructed him to build an ark. Noah was to gather his family and pairs of every kind of animal, both clean and unclean, and bring them into the ark to be saved from the flood.

Noah obeyed God's command and spent many years building the massive ark according to God's specific instructions. The ark was constructed with three decks, and its dimensions were 300 cubits long, 50 cubits wide, and 30 cubits high.

Once the ark was complete, Noah and his family, along with the animals, entered the ark, and God shut the door. Then, rain fell upon the earth for forty days and forty nights. The floodwaters rose, covering the entire earth, and even the highest mountains were submerged.

For 150 days, the floodwaters prevailed on the earth. Every living thing outside the ark perished, but Noah and those with him were safe inside. God remembered Noah and caused the floodwaters to recede.

After the floodwaters began to subside, Noah sent out a raven and a dove to see if the waters had receded from the earth. The dove returned with an olive leaf, indicating that the waters had sufficiently receded. Noah waited for another week and then sent the dove out again, and it did not return. This signified that the earth was dry.

God commanded Noah and his family to leave the ark and release all the animals. Noah built an altar and offered sacrifices to God as an act of worship and thanksgiving. God was pleased with Noah's sacrifice and made a covenant with him, promising never to destroy the earth by a flood again. As a sign of this covenant, God set a rainbow in the sky.

Noah and his family then began to repopulate the earth. They became the ancestors of all future generations. Noah lived for many years after the flood, and his story serves as a reminder of God's judgment, mercy, and faithfulness.

David and Goliath: A Giant Challenge

Once upon a time, in a land called Israel, there lived a young shepherd boy named David. He had a heart full of courage and a deep faith in God. David loved taking care of his father's sheep and spending time playing his harp, praising God with joyful songs.

One day, news spread across the land that a mighty warrior named Goliath was terrorizing the Israelite army. Goliath was a giant, standing over nine feet tall! He wore a heavy armor and carried a massive spear. Goliath challenged the Israelites, boasting that if any one of them could defeat him in battle, the Philistines would become their servants.

The Israelite soldiers were scared and trembling. But when David heard about the giant's challenge, he felt a fire ignite within him. He said to himself, "How dare this giant defy the living God? I will face him and show everyone that God is with me!"

David's words reached the ears of King Saul, who called for him. David stood before the king and said, "Do not be afraid, for I will go and fight this giant."

Saul was astonished and replied, "But you are just a young boy, and Goliath is a seasoned warrior! How can you defeat him?"

David smiled and answered, "Your majesty, when I was taking care of my father's sheep, a lion and a bear came to attack the flock. I fought them off with God's help and defeated them. The same God who saved me from the lion and the bear will save me from this giant too!"

Seeing David's faith and determination, King Saul agreed. He gave David his own armor, but it was too big and heavy for him. So David took it off and instead picked up his shepherd's staff and chose five smooth stones from a nearby stream. He placed them in his shepherd's bag and held his slingshot, ready for battle.

As David approached Goliath, the giant sneered and laughed. "Am I a dog that you come to me with sticks?" Goliath mocked.

David stood tall and replied, "You come to me with a sword and a spear, but I come to you in the name of the Lord Almighty, the God of Israel!"

With all his strength, David loaded a stone into his slingshot and swung it around, releasing it with precision. The stone soared through the air and struck Goliath right in the forehead. The giant stumbled and fell to the ground, defeated.

The Philistine army watched in shock as their champion was defeated by a young shepherd boy. The Israelites rejoiced and praised God for His mighty deliverance. David proved that with faith in God, even the most enormous challenges could be overcome.

From that day forward, David became known throughout the land as a brave and wise leader. He eventually became the beloved king of Israel, and his story continued to inspire people for generations to come.

Daniel in the Lion's Den

Once upon a time, in the land of Babylon, there lived a young man named Daniel. Daniel loved God with all his heart and followed His commandments faithfully. He was known for his wisdom and his unwavering trust in God.

In Babylon, there was a powerful king named Darius. He appointed many officials to help him rule over the land. Daniel was one of those officials because the king recognized his wisdom and integrity.

The other officials were jealous of Daniel's success and sought to bring him down. They plotted together and devised a plan to trick King Darius. They convinced the king to issue a decree stating that for thirty days, anyone who prayed to any god or man other than the king would be thrown into a den of hungry lions.

Now, Daniel knew about this decree, but he did not let fear control him. He continued to pray to God three times a day, just as he had always done. His love and trust in God were stronger than his fear of the lions.

When the jealous officials saw Daniel praying to God, they rushed to King Darius and reminded him of his decree. The king realized that he had been tricked, and he was deeply saddened because he admired Daniel and did not want any harm to come to him. But the law of the land could not be changed.

Reluctantly, King Darius gave the order, and Daniel was thrown into the den of lions. The king said to Daniel, "May your God, whom you serve so faithfully, deliver you!"

As Daniel was lowered into the den, the king's heart was heavy with worry. He couldn't sleep that night and anxiously awaited the morning. At the first light of dawn, King Darius hurried to the lion's den, calling out, "Daniel, servant of the living God, has your God whom you serve so faithfully been able to rescue you from the lions?"

To everyone's astonishment, Daniel's voice echoed from the depths of the den, "O King, live forever! My God sent His angel and shut the lions' mouths. They have not hurt me because I was found innocent in His sight. My trust was in Him."

King Darius was overjoyed and gave orders for Daniel to be lifted out of the den. Not a scratch was found on Daniel because God had protected him from harm.

Realizing the power and greatness of the one true God, King Darius issued a new decree throughout his kingdom. He declared that the God of Daniel was the living God who would be worshipped and honored by all. Anyone who spoke against this God would face severe punishment.

From that day forward, Daniel continued to serve as an important advisor to the king. His faithfulness to God and his miraculous deliverance from the lion's den inspired all who heard his story. Daniel's unwavering trust in God teaches us that even in the face of danger, we can find courage knowing that God is with us.

And so, Daniel lived a long and blessed life, continuing to honor God and serve as an example of faith and righteousness for generations to come.

The Story of Moses: From Baby in the Basket to the Red Sea

Once upon a time, in the land of Egypt, there was a Pharaoh who was afraid of the Israelites. He thought they were becoming too numerous and too powerful. So, he ordered that all baby boys born to the Israelites be thrown into the river.

During this difficult time, a brave Israelite woman named Jochebed gave birth to a baby boy. She saw that her son was special and didn't want anything to happen to him. So, she came up with a plan to protect him.

Jochebed lovingly made a basket out of reeds and coated it with tar to make it waterproof. She gently placed her baby boy in the basket and then carefully hid it among the tall reeds along the edge of the river Nile. Jochebed's daughter, Miriam, kept watch nearby to make sure the baby would be safe.

Not long after, the daughter of Pharaoh came to the river to bathe. She noticed the basket among the reeds and sent one of her maids to bring it to her. When she opened the basket, she saw the beautiful baby boy and felt great compassion for him.

Miriam, who had been watching, approached the princess and asked, "Shall I go and find a Hebrew woman to nurse the baby for you?"

The princess agreed, and Miriam quickly ran to get her mother, Jochebed. When they brought the baby boy to the princess, she named him Moses, which means "drawn out," because he had been drawn out of the water.

Moses grew up in Pharaoh's palace as the princess' adopted son. He received a fine education and had many privileges, but deep inside, he always knew he was an Israelite.

As Moses grew older, he witnessed the harsh treatment of his fellow Israelites by the Egyptians. One day, he saw an Egyptian beating an Israelite slave. Filled with righteous anger, Moses defended the Israelite and ended up killing the Egyptian. Realizing what he had done, Moses fled from Egypt, fearing Pharaoh's punishment.

In the land of Midian, Moses met a priest named Jethro and married his daughter, Zipporah. He settled down and became a shepherd, tending to Jethro's flock.

One day, as Moses was leading the flock near Mount Horeb, he saw a burning bush that was not consumed by the fire. Curious, he approached the bush, and from it, God called out to him, saying, "Moses, Moses!"

God told Moses that He had seen the suffering of the Israelites in Egypt and that He had chosen Moses to lead His people out of slavery and into the Promised Land, a land flowing with milk and honey.

With God's guidance and miracles, Moses returned to Egypt and confronted Pharaoh, demanding that he let the Israelites go. But Pharaoh's heart was hardened, and he refused.

So, God sent ten plagues upon Egypt, each more severe than the last. The final plague was the death of the firstborn, but the Israelites were spared because they followed God's instructions. Pharaoh finally relented and allowed the Israelites to leave.

With Moses as their leader, the Israelites journeyed through the wilderness. God guided them with a pillar of cloud by day and a pillar of fire by night. When Pharaoh changed his mind and pursued them with his army, the Israelites found themselves trapped between the Egyptian army and the Red Sea.

But God performed another miracle. He parted the waters of the Red Sea, creating a dry path through the sea. The Israelites walked through on dry land, with walls of water on either side.

When Pharaoh's army attempted to follow, God caused the waters to crash down upon them, destroying the entire Egyptian army. The Israelites were free at last!

Moses and the Israelites rejoiced and praised God for His mighty deliverance. They continued their journey through the wilderness, facing challenges along the way, but always knowing that God was with them, leading them to the Promised Land.

And so, Moses, from being a baby in a basket to standing at the edge of the Red Sea, demonstrated great courage and obedience to God's calling. His story teaches us the importance of trusting in God's plan, even in the face of adversity.

The Parable of the Good Samaritan

Once upon a time, there was a traveler who was walking down a road. He was on his way to a distant city, but the journey was long and tiring. As he walked, he suddenly heard a cry for help coming from the side of the road.

Curious and concerned, the traveler hurried towards the sound. There, he saw a man lying on the ground, beaten and badly hurt. It was clear that he had been attacked by robbers and left to suffer.

The traveler felt compassion for the injured man. He knelt down beside him and gently asked, "Are you okay? Can I help you?"

The injured man weakly replied, "I've been attacked and left here. I'm in pain and I can't go on."

Without hesitation, the traveler decided to help. He carefully cleaned the man's wounds, bandaged them, and gave him water to drink. The traveler even lifted the injured man onto his own donkey and brought him to an inn nearby.

At the inn, the traveler spoke to the
innkeeper and said, "Please take care of this
man. Here is some money to cover his
expenses. If it costs more, I will pay you
back when I return."

The traveler stayed with the injured man
until he was sure that he would be taken
care of. Then, he continued his journey,
knowing that he had done a good deed.

Now, as the story goes, a priest happened to be walking down the same road. When he saw the injured man, he crossed to the other side and continued on his way. He ignored the cries for help and didn't stop to lend a hand.

Similarly, a Levite, who was supposed to be knowledgeable about the law of God, came by and saw the injured man. But he too passed by on the other side without offering any assistance.

However, it was a Samaritan, a person from a group despised by many in those times, who came by next. When he saw the injured man, he felt deep compassion. He didn't care about the differences between them or the prejudices of the world. The Samaritan immediately stopped and went to help.

He tended to the man's wounds, just like the traveler had done earlier. Then, the Samaritan lifted the injured man onto his donkey and brought him to the same inn. He even paid the innkeeper extra money and said, "Please take care of him. If there are any additional expenses, I will cover them when I return."

Jesus, who was telling this story to the people, then asked, "Which of these three men do you think was a neighbor to the man who was attacked?"

The people thought for a moment and replied, "The one who showed him mercy and helped him."

Jesus smiled and said, "You are correct. Go and do likewise. Show love and kindness to those who are in need, regardless of who they are. Be a good neighbor to all."

And so, the story of the Good Samaritan teaches us the importance of showing compassion, kindness, and love to everyone we meet. It reminds us that we should treat others as we would like to be treated ourselves.

The Birth of Jesus: A Special Night in Bethlehem

Once upon a time, in the town of Nazareth, there lived a young woman named Mary. She was a kind and gentle soul who loved God with all her heart. Mary was engaged to a man named Joseph, who was a carpenter.

One day, an angel named Gabriel appeared to Mary. The angel greeted her and said, "Do not be afraid, Mary, for you have found favor with God. You will conceive and give birth to a son, and you are to call him Jesus. He will be great and will be called the Son of the Most High."

Mary was surprised and wondered how this could be, for she was not yet married. But the angel reassured her, saying, "The Holy Spirit will come upon you, and the power of the Most High will overshadow you. The child to be born will be holy; he will be called the Son of God."

Filled with faith and trust in God, Mary
humbly replied, "I am the Lord's servant.
May everything you have said come true."
And from that moment, Mary carried the
baby Jesus within her womb.

A short while later, a decree came from the ruler of the land, Caesar Augustus. He ordered that a census be taken, and everyone had to return to their hometown to be counted. Joseph, being from the house of David, had to travel to Bethlehem, the city of David.

Mary and Joseph embarked on a long journey to Bethlehem. They traveled by foot, and Mary, being heavily pregnant, found it quite challenging. But they trusted in God's plan and knew that He would take care of them.

When they finally arrived in Bethlehem, the town was crowded with people who had come for the census. Finding a place to stay became difficult. Mary and Joseph desperately sought shelter, but all the inns were full.

An innkeeper saw their weary faces and offered them a stable where animals were kept. Grateful for any place to rest, Mary and Joseph entered the humble stable. It was a simple and quiet place, far from the comfort of home.

That night, in the humble stable of Bethlehem, Mary gave birth to her son, Jesus. She wrapped Him in swaddling clothes and laid Him in a manger, a feeding trough for animals. It was an unusual place for a baby, but Mary and Joseph rejoiced in the miracle of His birth.

Out in the fields nearby, shepherds were tending their sheep. Suddenly, an angel of the Lord appeared to them, surrounded by a heavenly light. The shepherds were frightened, but the angel said, "Do not be afraid! I bring you good news of great joy for all people. Today in the town of David, a Savior has been born to you; He is the Messiah, the Lord."

As the shepherds listened in awe, a multitude of angels appeared, praising God and saying, "Glory to God in the highest, and on earth peace, goodwill toward men!"

Filled with wonder and excitement, the shepherds hurried to Bethlehem to see the baby Jesus. They found Mary, Joseph, and the baby, just as the angel had said. They knelt before the manger, offering their love and worship to the newborn King.

In that quiet stable, surrounded by love and adoration, the promised Messiah had come into the world. Jesus, the Son of God, brought hope, peace, and salvation to all people.

And so, on that special night in Bethlehem, the humble birth of Jesus marked the beginning of a new era—a time of joy, forgiveness, and God's eternal love. The story of Jesus' birth reminds us of the greatest gift we have received and teaches us to cherish the true meaning of Christmas.

Jonah and the Big Fish

Once upon a time, there was a man named Jonah. God chose Jonah to be a prophet and gave him an important task to do. God said to Jonah, "Go to the great city of Nineveh and tell the people there to turn away from their wickedness."

But Jonah did not want to go to Nineveh. Instead, he decided to run away from God. He thought he could escape from God's presence by going in a different direction. Jonah found a ship heading to a faraway place called Tarshish and boarded it, hoping to leave God's command behind.

While Jonah was on the ship, a powerful storm suddenly arose. The wind howled, and the waves crashed against the boat. The sailors on the ship were terrified, thinking they would sink. Each one cried out to their gods for help.

Meanwhile, Jonah was down in the ship's hold, fast asleep. The captain woke him up and said, "How can you sleep? Pray to your God! Maybe He will save us from this disaster!"

The sailors cast lots to determine who was responsible for the storm, and the lot fell on Jonah. They questioned him about his background, and Jonah confessed, saying, "I am a Hebrew, and I worship the Lord, the God of heaven, who made the sea and the dry land."

Terrified by Jonah's words, the sailors asked him what they should do to stop the storm. Jonah told them, "Throw me into the sea, and the storm will calm down. It's because of me that this is happening."

Reluctantly, the sailors threw Jonah into the sea. As soon as Jonah hit the water, the storm instantly stopped. The sailors were amazed at the power of Jonah's God.

But God was not finished with Jonah. He sent a great fish to swallow Jonah and save him from drowning. Inside the belly of the fish, Jonah realized his mistake and cried out to God for help. He prayed and repented, promising to obey God's command.

God heard Jonah's prayer and commanded the fish to spit Jonah out onto dry land. The fish obeyed, and Jonah found himself standing on the shore.

Once again, God spoke to Jonah and said, "Go to Nineveh and deliver my message to the people." This time, Jonah obeyed without hesitation. He walked through the city, proclaiming, "Forty days more and Nineveh will be overthrown!"

Surprisingly, the people of Nineveh believed Jonah's message. They turned away from their wickedness and began to pray to God for forgiveness. Even the king declared a fast and ordered everyone to repent.

Seeing the people's sincere repentance, God decided not to destroy Nineveh. He showed them mercy and spared the city.

Jonah, however, was not happy with this outcome. He became angry at God's compassion towards the people of Nineveh. But God taught Jonah a valuable lesson about love, forgiveness, and His desire for all people to turn to Him.

And so, the story of Jonah and the big fish teaches us about God's unfailing love, His willingness to forgive, and the importance of obeying His commands. It reminds us that we cannot run away from God's presence, and when we repent and turn to Him, He is always ready to show us mercy.

The Ten Plagues of Egypt

Once upon a time, in the land of Egypt, there was a powerful ruler called Pharaoh. Pharaoh was not kind to the Israelites, who were living in Egypt as slaves. God saw their suffering and decided to set His people free.

To accomplish this, God chose a man named Moses to be His messenger. God told Moses to go to Pharaoh and demand the release of the Israelites. Moses obeyed God's command and went to the palace.

When Moses spoke to Pharaoh and asked him to let the Israelites go, Pharaoh stubbornly refused. He did not want to lose the labor force that the Israelites provided. So, God sent a series of ten miraculous plagues upon Egypt to convince Pharaoh to free the Israelites.

The first plague was turning the Nile River into blood. The once clean and life-giving water turned into a river of blood, making it undrinkable. But Pharaoh's heart remained hard, and he did not listen to Moses.

The second plague was a swarm of frogs. Frogs filled the land, entering houses and even Pharaoh's palace. They were everywhere, causing great distress to the Egyptians. Moses pleaded with Pharaoh to let the Israelites go, but Pharaoh still refused.

The third plague was an infestation of gnats. These tiny insects covered the land, causing annoyance and discomfort to the Egyptians. Despite the gnats, Pharaoh did not change his mind.

The fourth plague was a swarm of flies. Flies filled the air, covering the land of Egypt. They were everywhere, but they did not come near the land where the Israelites lived. Even though the flies were a nuisance, Pharaoh's heart remained stubborn.

The fifth plague brought a deadly disease upon the livestock of Egypt. All the horses, donkeys, camels, and other animals owned by the Egyptians became sick and died. Yet, Pharaoh's heart remained hard, and he did not let the Israelites go.

The sixth plague was painful boils that broke out on the skin of the Egyptians and their animals. The boils caused great suffering and pain, but Pharaoh still did not listen to Moses.

The seventh plague was a devastating hailstorm. Hail, mixed with fire, rained down upon Egypt. It destroyed crops, trees, and everything in its path. Some Egyptians were afraid and pleaded with Pharaoh to release the Israelites, but Pharaoh's heart remained stubborn.

The eighth plague brought a swarm of locusts. These insects devoured every green thing that remained after the hailstorm. They covered the land, leaving it barren and desolate. Pharaoh's advisers begged him to let the Israelites go, but he refused once again.

The ninth plague brought darkness upon the land of Egypt. For three days, darkness covered the entire land, so thick that the Egyptians couldn't see anything. Yet, Pharaoh still did not release the Israelites.

Finally, God sent the tenth and most terrible plague—the death of the firstborn. God told the Israelites to mark their doors with the blood of a lamb, so the Angel of Death would pass over their homes. But in every Egyptian household, the firstborn child and even the firstborn animals died.

This last plague broke Pharaoh's resistance. He was grief-stricken by the loss and summoned Moses and Aaron. Pharaoh finally agreed to let the Israelites go.

And so, with the ten plagues, God showed His power and delivered His people from slavery in Egypt. The Israelites left Egypt and began their journey towards the Promised Land, free at last.

The story of the ten plagues teaches us about God's justice, mercy, and faithfulness. It shows us that God will go to great lengths to rescue His people and fulfill His promises. It reminds us to trust in God's power and follow His guidance in our own lives.

Thank you

We wanted to take a moment to express our deepest gratitude for your recent purchase of our books written by our beloved author of kids' stories. Your support and appreciation mean the world to us and serve as a heartwarming affirmation of the hard work and passion that goes into creating these magical tales.

Every word, every character, and every adventure within those pages were crafted with the intention of sparking imaginations, igniting curiosity, and nurturing a love for reading in young minds. It brings us immense joy to know that our stories have found a place in the hearts and homes of children across the world.

We hope that the books you purchased bring endless smiles, laughter, and cherished moments shared between parents and their children. We would be honored if you would consider sharing your thoughts and experiences with us. Your feedback not only helps us improve but also serves as a source of motivation to create more captivating stories in the future.

Printed in the USA
CPSIA information can be obtained
at www.ICGtesting.com
LVHW071658200124
769095LV00002B/44

9 781803 935331